Teach Your Child to Read

# 300 Short Easy Sentences

*English - Hungarian*

1

## I Can...

- [ ] read the 1st sentence.
- [ ] read the 2nd sentence.
- [ ] make a sentence from a picture.
- [ ] color a picture.
- [ ] Draw a picture.

The frog is going to a party.

A béka partira megy.

The happy frog is wearing a green hat.

A boldog béka zöld kalapot visel.

# Name

## I Can...

- [ ] read the 1st sentence.
- [ ] read the 2nd sentence.
- [ ] make a sentence from a picture.
- [ ] color a picture.
- [ ] Draw a picture.

Owl likes to read big books.

Bagoly szeret nagy könyveket olvasni.

A smart owl is reading an alphabet book.

Egy intelligens bagoly ábécé könyvet olvas.

Name

## I Can...

- [ ] read the 1st sentence.
- [ ] read the 2nd sentence.
- [ ] make a sentence from a picture.
- [ ] color a picture.
- [ ] Draw a picture.

Come on! The ice cream truck is here!

Gyerünk! Itt van a fagylalt teherautó!

He is driving a big icecream truck.

Nagy fagylaltot szállít.

Name

## I Can...

- [ ] read the 1st sentence.
- [ ] read the 2nd sentence.
- [ ] make a sentence from a picture.
- [ ] color a picture.
- [ ] Draw a picture.

Dragons are very friendly and have scales on their backs.

A sárkányok nagyon barátságosak és mérlegek vannak a hátukon.

The dragon is waving his hand.

A sárkány integetett a kezével.

Name

## I Can...

- [ ] read the 1st sentence.
- [ ] read the 2nd sentence.
- [ ] make a sentence from a picture.
- [ ] color a picture.
- [ ] Draw a picture.

This ram lives in the farmhouse.

Ez a kos él a parasztházban.

Ram has a large horn and fluffy wool.

A Ramnak nagy szarv és bolyhos gyapjú van.

Name

## I Can…

- [ ] read the 1st sentence.
- [ ] read the 2nd sentence.
- [ ] make a sentence from a picture.
- [ ] color a picture.
- [ ] Draw a picture.

The bunny likes to eat carrots.

A nyuszi szeret sárgarépát enni.

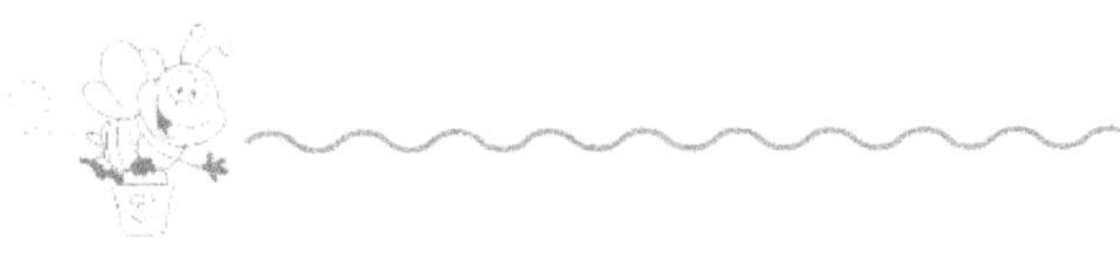

Rabbit thinks that the juicy orange carrot looks yummy.

Nyúl szerint a lédús narancs sárgarépa finomnak tűnik.

Name

## I Can...

- [ ] read the 1st sentence.
- [ ] read the 2nd sentence.
- [ ] make a sentence from a picture.
- [ ] color a picture.
- [ ] Draw a picture.

The clown likes to give out balloons to little kids.

A bohóc szereti léggömbök kiadását a kisgyermekek számára.

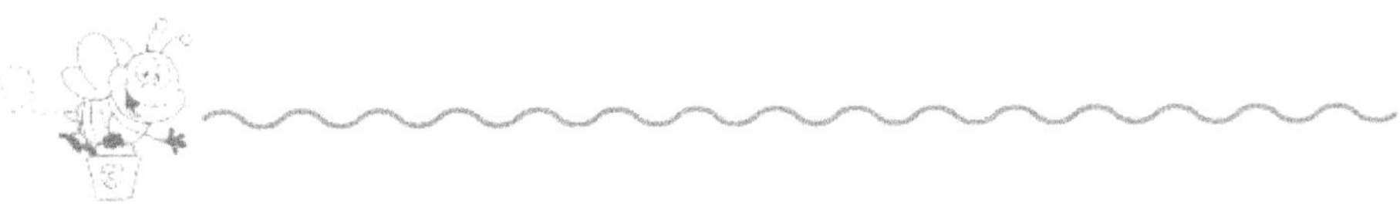

Funny, Mr. Clown is giving away colorful balloons.

Vicces, Mr. Bohóc színes léggömböket ad el.

Name ______________________ 

## I Can...

- [ ] read the 1st sentence.
- [ ] read the 2nd sentence.
- [ ] make a sentence from a picture.
- [ ] color a picture.
- [ ] Draw a picture.

The clown is juggling balls for his performance.

A bohóc golyókat zsongál a teljesítményéért.

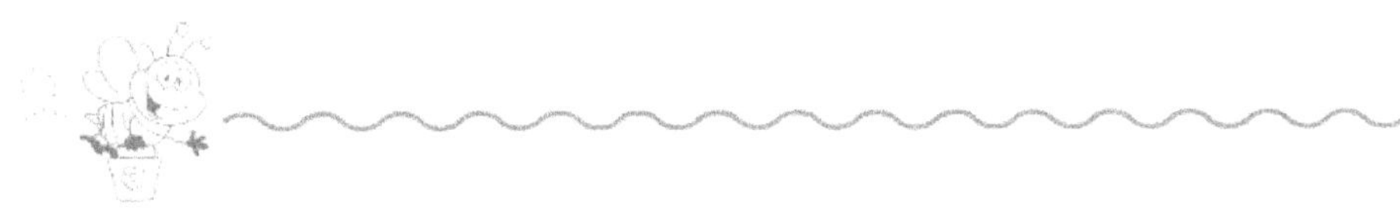

Talented, Mr. Clown is juggling five red balls.

Lehetséges, Mr. Bohóc öt piros golyót zsonglőr.

Name ___________________ 

## I Can...

- [ ] read the 1st sentence.
- [ ] read the 2nd sentence.
- [ ] make a sentence from a picture.
- [ ] color a picture.
- [ ] Draw a picture.

The Easter Bunny is going to give out chocolate eggs.

A húsvéti nyuszi csokoládétojást fog adni.

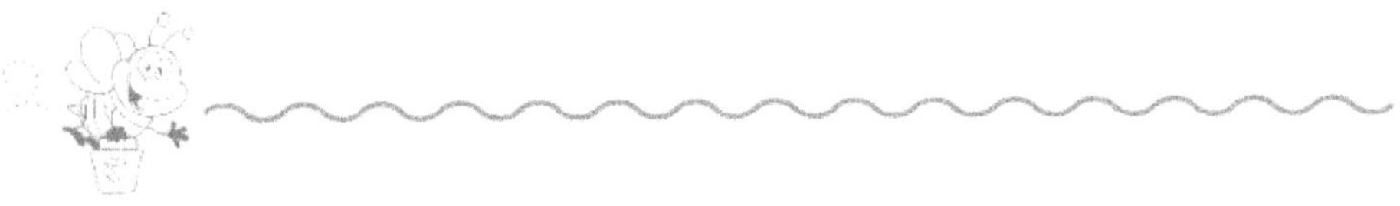

The rabbit goes out to buy more orange carrots.

A nyúl megy ki, hogy több narancssárga sárgarépát vásároljon.

# Name _______________ 

## I Can...

- [ ] read the 1st sentence.
- [ ] read the 2nd sentence.
- [ ] make a sentence from a picture.
- [ ] color a picture.
- [ ] Draw a picture.

The pencil is drawing a zig-zag line.

A ceruza cikcakk vonalat rajzol.

The Pencil is saying hello to you.

A Ceru köszönt neked.

Name

## I Can...

- [ ] read the 1st sentence.
- [ ] read the 2nd sentence.
- [ ] make a sentence from a picture.
- [ ] color a picture.
- [ ] Draw a picture.

The pencil put on a big smile and went to work.

A ceruza elmosolyodott, és elment dolgozni.

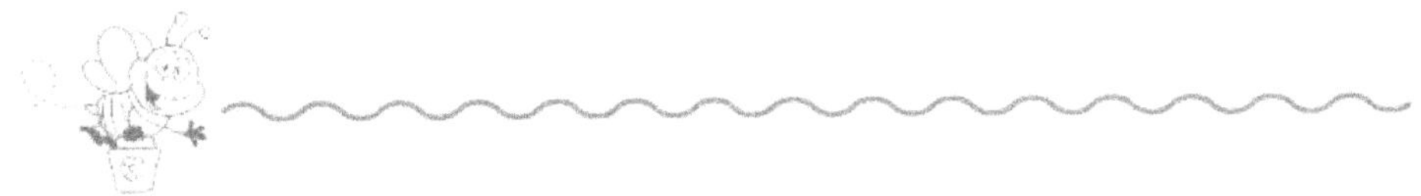

The Pencil is leaving to go on a long relaxing vacation.

A Ceruza elmegy hosszú pihentető nyaralásra.

Name _______________________

This snowman is my friend, and he is a helper of Santa.

Ez a hóember a barátom, és a Mikulás segítője.

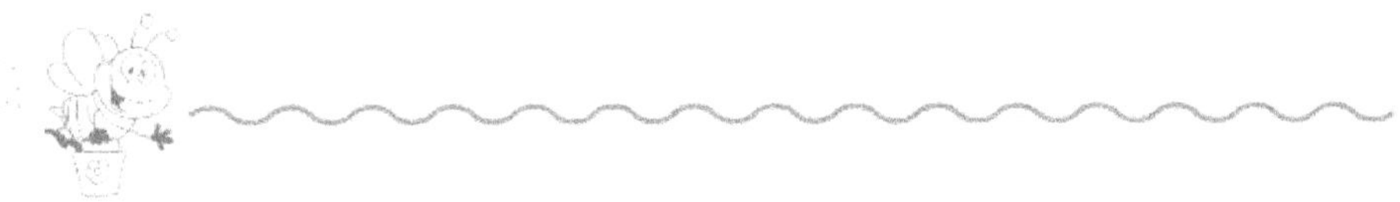

Mr. Snowman is celebrating Christmas by the decorated tree.

Hóember ünnepli a karácsonyt a díszített fa alatt.

Name 

## I Can...

- [ ] read the 1st sentence.
- [ ] read the 2nd sentence.
- [ ] make a sentence from a picture.
- [ ] color a picture.
- [ ] Draw a picture.

The octopus is working as a chef and serving food.

A polip szakácsként dolgozik és ételt szolgál fel.

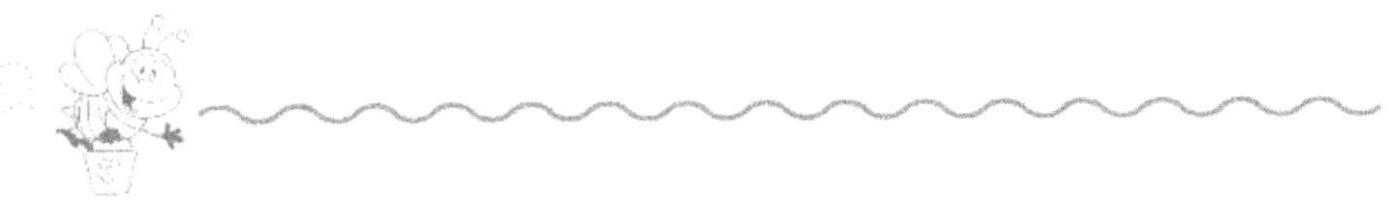

Chef Octopus is serving a delicious turkey dinner.

A Octopus séf finom pulykavacsorát szolgál fel.

# Name

## I Can...

- [ ] read the 1st sentence.
- [ ] read the 2nd sentence.
- [ ] make a sentence from a picture.
- [ ] color a picture.
- [ ] Draw a picture.

Santa is happy.

Télapó boldog.

Santa Claus is giving extraordinary presents to excited kids.

A Mikulás rendkívüli ajándékokat ad az izgatott gyerekeknek.

Name

# I Can...

- [ ] read the 1st sentence.
- [ ] read the 2nd sentence.
- [ ] make a sentence from a picture.
- [ ] color a picture.
- [ ] Draw a picture.

The bear likes to eat sweets.

A medve szeret enni édességeket.

Teddy is licking a red and white candy cane.

Teddy nyal egy vörös és fehér cukorkát.

Name

## I Can...

- [ ] read the 1st sentence.
- [ ] read the 2nd sentence.
- [ ] make a sentence from a picture.
- [ ] color a picture.
- [ ] Draw a picture.

The book has a wand.

A könyvnek pálcája van.

The cereal box got a magician set for Christmas.

A gabona dobozban máguskészlet került karácsonyra.

Name

## I Can...

- [ ] read the 1st sentence.
- [ ] read the 2nd sentence.
- [ ] make a sentence from a picture.
- [ ] color a picture.
- [ ] Draw a picture.

The bear has a present.

A medvenek van ajándéka.

Happy Teddy is opening his box of presents from Santa.

Happy Teddy kinyitja a télapó ajándék dobozát.

Name 

## I Can...

- [ ] read the 1st sentence.
- [ ] read the 2nd sentence.
- [ ] make a sentence from a picture.
- [ ] color a picture.
- [ ] Draw a picture.

Santa is going to give out presents.

A télapó ajándékokat fog adni.

 ~~~~~~~~~~~~~~~~~~~~~~~~~~~~~~~~~~~~~~~~

Santa is lugging a large brown bag of gifts to his sley.

Télapó nagy barna ajándékcsomagot húz a vállához.

Name ___________

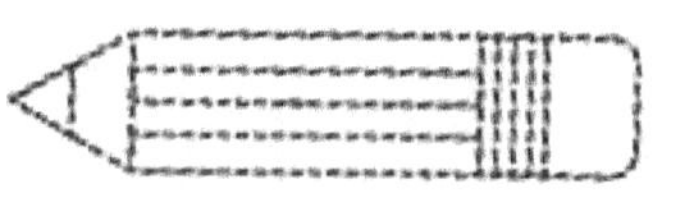

## I Can...

- [ ] read the 1st sentence.
- [ ] read the 2nd sentence.
- [ ] make a sentence from a picture.
- [ ] color a picture.
- [ ] Draw a picture.

I made a snowman.

Csináltam egy hóember.

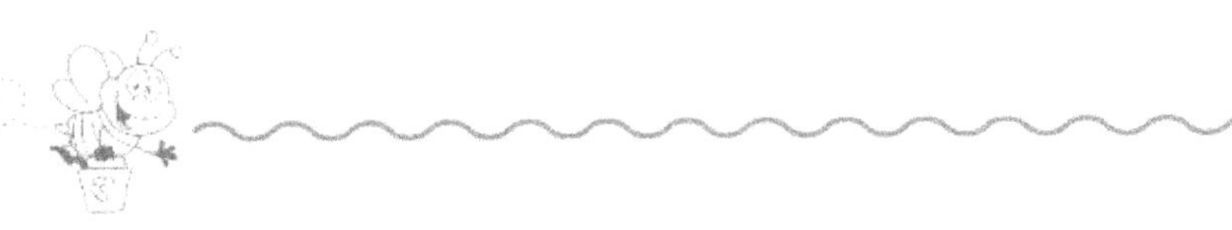

Mr. Snowman is holding a broom and saying goodbye.

Hóember tart egy seprűt, és búcsút mond.

Name

## I Can...

- ☐ read the 1st sentence.
- ☐ read the 2nd sentence.
- ☐ make a sentence from a picture.
- ☐ color a picture.
- ☐ Draw a picture.

The parrot is colorful.

A papagáj színes.

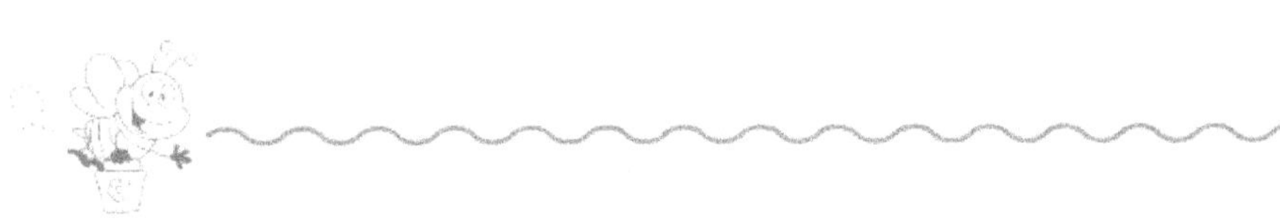

The green parrot came from the forest to the zoo.

A zöld papagáj az erdőből jött az állatkertbe.

Name

## I Can...

- [ ] read the 1st sentence.
- [ ] read the 2nd sentence.
- [ ] make a sentence from a picture.
- [ ] color a picture.
- [ ] Draw a picture.

There are a lot of animals.

Nagyon sok állat van.

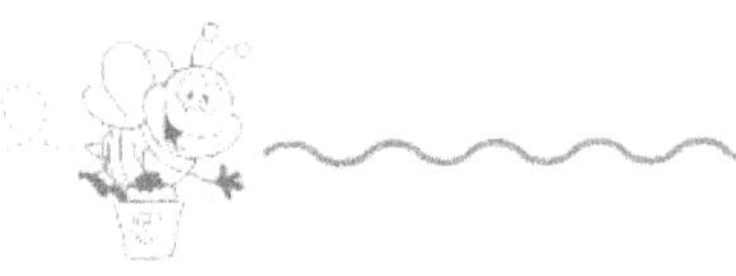

The animals are happy being together again.

Az állatok örülnek, hogy újra együtt vannak.

# Name

## I Can...

- [ ] read the 1st sentence.
- [ ] read the 2nd sentence.
- [ ] make a sentence from a picture.
- [ ] color a picture.
- [ ] Draw a picture.

The man is wearing a belt.

Az ember övet visel.

_______________________

The carpenter is fixing something.

Az asztalos javít valamit.

Name

## I Can...

- [ ] read the 1st sentence.
- [ ] read the 2nd sentence.
- [ ] make a sentence from a picture.
- [ ] color a picture.
- [ ] Draw a picture.

The rabbit is very young.

A nyúl nagyon fiatal.

The magician plays a trick.

A mágus egy trükköt játszik.

Name _______________

## I Can...

- ☐ read the 1st sentence.
- ☐ read the 2nd sentence.
- ☐ make a sentence from a picture.
- ☐ color a picture.
- ☐ Draw a picture.

He has a potion.

Van egy bájital.

 ~~~~~~~~~~~~~~~~~~~~~~~~~~~~~~

The scientist is making a potion.

A tudós főz.

Name 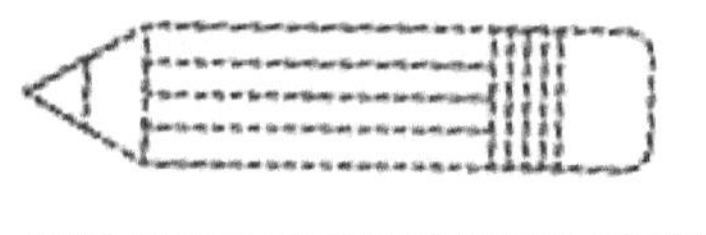

## I Can...

- [ ] read the 1st sentence.
- [ ] read the 2nd sentence.
- [ ] make a sentence from a picture.
- [ ] color a picture.
- [ ] Draw a picture.

He is wearing sunglasses.

Napszemüveget visel.

The policeman is mad.

A rendőr őrült.

Name

## I Can...

- [ ] read the 1st sentence.
- [ ] read the 2nd sentence.
- [ ] make a sentence from a picture.
- [ ] color a picture.
- [ ] Draw a picture.

He has a bucket of paint.

Van egy vödör festék.

He likes to paint.

Szeret festeni.

Name ___________________

## I Can...

- [ ] read the 1st sentence.
- [ ] read the 2nd sentence.
- [ ] make a sentence from a picture.
- [ ] color a picture.
- [ ] Draw a picture.

The man has a hat.

Az embernek van kalapja.

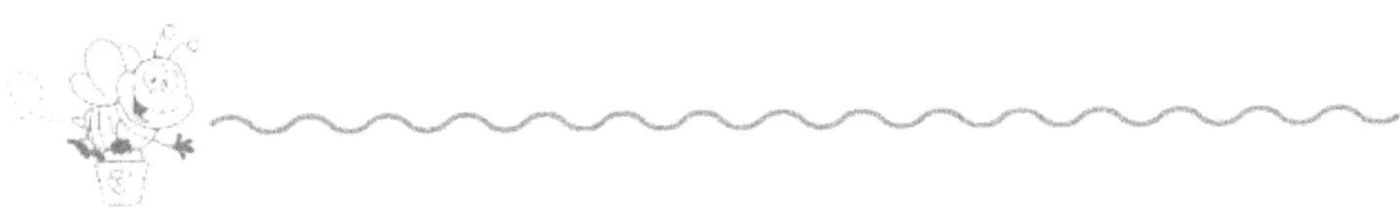

The postman is giving out the mail in the early morning.

A postás kora reggel kiadja a postát.

Name

## I Can...

- [ ] read the 1st sentence.
- [ ] read the 2nd sentence.
- [ ] make a sentence from a picture.
- [ ] color a picture.
- [ ] Draw a picture.

He has a walkie talkie.

Van egy walkie-talkie.

He is going to work with his suitcase.

A bőröndjével fog dolgozni.

Name

## I Can...

- [ ] read the 1st sentence.
- [ ] read the 2nd sentence.
- [ ] make a sentence from a picture.
- [ ] color a picture.
- [ ] Draw a picture.

He is sleepy.

Álmos.

The delivery man sent us a package.

A kézbesítő küldött nekünk egy csomagot.

Name

## I Can...

- [ ] read the 1st sentence.
- [ ] read the 2nd sentence.
- [ ] make a sentence from a picture.
- [ ] color a picture.
- [ ] Draw a picture.

He is wearing a bowtie.

Nyakkendőt visel.

The waiter is serving juice.

A pincér juice szolgál.

Name

## I Can...

- [ ] read the 1st sentence.
- [ ] read the 2nd sentence.
- [ ] make a sentence from a picture.
- [ ] color a picture.
- [ ] Draw a picture.

He has a suitcase.

Van egy bőröndje.

The engineer is holding a wrench.

A mérnök csavarkulcsot tart.

Name

## I Can...

- [ ] read the 1st sentence.
- [ ] read the 2nd sentence.
- [ ] make a sentence from a picture.
- [ ] color a picture.
- [ ] Draw a picture.

The chef has a napkin.

A séfnek van egy szalvéta.

The chef serves delicious-looking food.

A séf finom kinézetű ételeket szolgál fel.

Name

## I Can...

- [ ] read the 1st sentence.
- [ ] read the 2nd sentence.
- [ ] make a sentence from a picture.
- [ ] color a picture.
- [ ] Draw a picture.

The rooster has a big beak.

A kakasnak nagy a csőr.

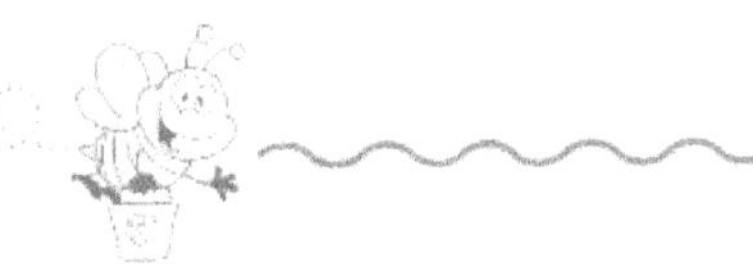

The chicken is saying hello to us.

A csirke köszön, nekünk.

Name

## I Can...

- [ ] read the 1st sentence.
- [ ] read the 2nd sentence.
- [ ] make a sentence from a picture.
- [ ] color a picture.
- [ ] Draw a picture.

The bird is small.

A madár kicsi.

The chick is on the telephone talking with his friend.

A csaj telefonon beszél a barátjával.

Name

## I Can...

- [ ] read the 1st sentence.
- [ ] read the 2nd sentence.
- [ ] make a sentence from a picture.
- [ ] color a picture.
- [ ] Draw a picture.

That is my ring.

Ez a gyűrűm.

That is a beautiful ring.

Ez egy gyönyörű gyűrű.

The duck has three eggs.

A kacsanak három tojása van.

The duck has a big nose.

A kacsa nagy orrú.

Name

## I Can...

- [ ] read the 1st sentence.
- [ ] read the 2nd sentence.
- [ ] make a sentence from a picture.
- [ ] color a picture.
- [ ] Draw a picture.

The swan is beautiful.

A hattyú gyönyörű.

The graceful swan is striding through the water.

A kecses hattyú átvág a vízen.

Name

## I Can...

- [ ] read the 1st sentence.
- [ ] read the 2nd sentence.
- [ ] make a sentence from a picture.
- [ ] color a picture.
- [ ] Draw a picture.

The girl is wearing a dress.

A lány ruhát visel.

The maid is cleaning our room.

A szobalány takarítja a szobánkat.

Name ___________________

## I Can...

- [ ] read the 1st sentence.
- [ ] read the 2nd sentence.
- [ ] make a sentence from a picture.
- [ ] color a picture.
- [ ] Draw a picture.

The boy is running.

A fiú fut.

_______________________________

The little boy was running.

A kisfiú futott.

Name

## I Can...

- [ ] read the 1st sentence.
- [ ] read the 2nd sentence.
- [ ] make a sentence from a picture.
- [ ] color a picture.
- [ ] Draw a picture.

He is a musician.

Zenész.

He is playing a lively tune on his flute.

Élő dallamot játszik a furulán.

Name

## I Can...

- [ ] read the 1st sentence.
- [ ] read the 2nd sentence.
- [ ] make a sentence from a picture.
- [ ] color a picture.
- [ ] Draw a picture.

He looks joyful.

Örömmel néz ki.

That boy works in a band and plays the drum.

Ez a fiú zenekarban dolgozik és dobot játszik.

Name

## I Can...

- [ ] read the 1st sentence.
- [ ] read the 2nd sentence.
- [ ] make a sentence from a picture.
- [ ] color a picture.
- [ ] Draw a picture.

The dinosaur is a rock star.

A dinoszaurusz egy rocksztár.

The dragon is playing the guitar.

A sárkány gitározik.

Name

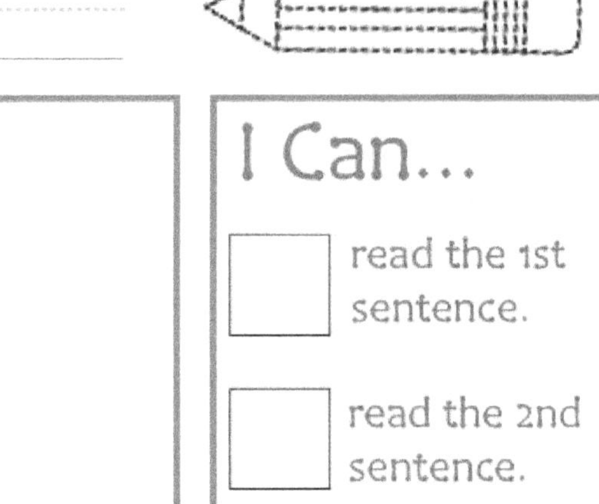

## I Can...

- [ ] read the 1st sentence.
- [ ] read the 2nd sentence.
- [ ] make a sentence from a picture.
- [ ] color a picture.
- [ ] Draw a picture.

The nurse helps the doctor.

A nővér segít az orvosnak.

The nurse looks scary, holding a syringe.

A nővér félelmetesnek tűnik, fecskendővel tartva.

Name

## I Can...

- [ ] read the 1st sentence.
- [ ] read the 2nd sentence.
- [ ] make a sentence from a picture.
- [ ] color a picture.
- [ ] Draw a picture.

She is wearing a crown.

Koronát visel.

The queen bee has a beautiful wand.

A méhkirálynőnek gyönyörű pálca van.

Name

## I Can...

- [ ] read the 1st sentence.
- [ ] read the 2nd sentence.
- [ ] make a sentence from a picture.
- [ ] color a picture.
- [ ] Draw a picture.

It is orange and black.

Narancssárga és fekete.

The tiger is wearing a bow on its neck.

A tigris íjat visel a nyakán.

Name

## I Can...

- [ ] read the 1st sentence.
- [ ] read the 2nd sentence.
- [ ] make a sentence from a picture.
- [ ] color a picture.
- [ ] Draw a picture.

The boy is carrying a lot of books.

A fiú sok könyvet szállít.

The boy is carrying so many books!

A fiú olyan sok könyvet hordoz!

Name

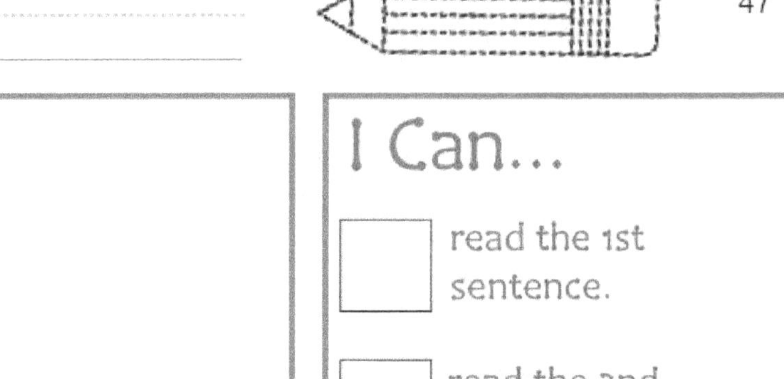

## I Can...

- [ ] read the 1st sentence.
- [ ] read the 2nd sentence.
- [ ] make a sentence from a picture.
- [ ] color a picture.
- [ ] Draw a picture.

The pizza looks delicious.

A pizza finomnak tűnik.

The waiter is serving steaming hot pizza.

A pincér forró pizzát szolgál fel.

Name ____________________

## I Can...

- ☐ read the 1st sentence.
- ☐ read the 2nd sentence.
- ☐ make a sentence from a picture.
- ☐ color a picture.
- ☐ Draw a picture.

That is my dad's computer.

Az apám számítógépe.

 ~~~~~~~~~~~~~~~~~~~~~~~~~

My dad works on the computer.

Apám számítógépen dolgozik.

Name

## I Can...

- [ ] read the 1st sentence.
- [ ] read the 2nd sentence.
- [ ] make a sentence from a picture.
- [ ] color a picture.
- [ ] Draw a picture.

The farmer has a beard.

A gazdanak szakálla van.

The gardener is going to plant flowers

A kertész virágot fog ültetni

Name

## I Can...

- [ ] read the 1st sentence.
- [ ] read the 2nd sentence.
- [ ] make a sentence from a picture.
- [ ] color a picture.
- [ ] Draw a picture.

The strawberry is red.

Az eper vörös.

I love to drink strawberry juice.

Szeretek inni eper juice-t.

# Name

## I Can...

- [ ] read the 1st sentence.
- [ ] read the 2nd sentence.
- [ ] make a sentence from a picture.
- [ ] color a picture.
- [ ] Draw a picture.

The magician has a wand.

A mágusnak pálcája van.

The wizard likes to work with magic.

A varázsló szereti a varázslatot.

## I Can...

- [ ] read the 1st sentence.
- [ ] read the 2nd sentence.
- [ ] make a sentence from a picture.
- [ ] color a picture.
- [ ] Draw a picture.

Reindeer has a scarf.

A rénszarvasnak sála van.

~~~~~~~~~~~~~~~~~~~~~~~~~~~~~~~~~~~~~~~~~~~~~~~~~~~

Santa gave reindeer a big present.

A télapó nagy ajándékot adott a rénszarvasnak.
~~~~~~~~~~~~~~~~~~~~~~~~~~~~~~~~~~~~~~~~~~~~~~~~~~~

Name

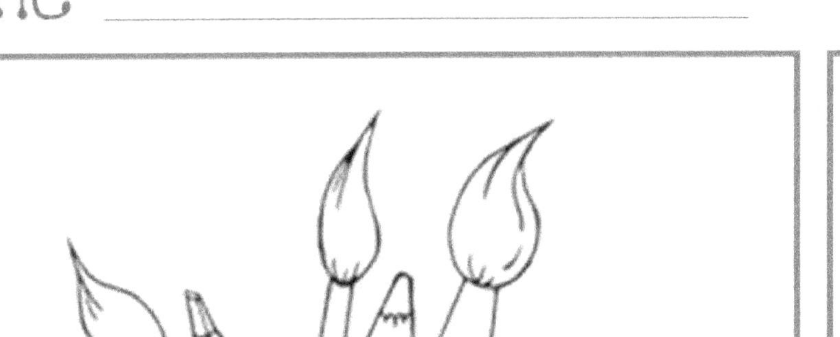

## I Can...

- [ ] read the 1st sentence.
- [ ] read the 2nd sentence.
- [ ] make a sentence from a picture.
- [ ] color a picture.
- [ ] Draw a picture.

I have a lot of pencils.

Nagyon sok ceruza van.

I have a lot of brushes and pencils.

Nagyon sok kefe és ceruza van.

Name _______________

## I Can...

- ☐ read the 1st sentence.
- ☐ read the 2nd sentence.
- ☐ make a sentence from a picture.
- ☐ color a picture.
- ☐ Draw a picture.

Santa is fat.

A Mikulás kövér.

 ~~~~~~~~~~~~~~~~~~~~~~~~~~~

Santa is having fun.

I élapó szórakozik.

Name 

## I Can...

- [ ] read the 1st sentence.
- [ ] read the 2nd sentence.
- [ ] make a sentence from a picture.
- [ ] color a picture.
- [ ] Draw a picture.

I have one nose.

Van egy orrom.

The one is saying its name.

Az egyik a nevét mondja.

## I Can...

- [ ] read the 1st sentence.
- [ ] read the 2nd sentence.
- [ ] make a sentence from a picture.
- [ ] color a picture.
- [ ] Draw a picture.

I have two ears.

Két fülem van.

 ~~~~~~~~~~~~~~~~~~~~~~~~~~~~~~~~~~~~

The number "two" is holding up bunny ears.

A "két" szám feltartja a nyuszi füleit.

Name ______________________

## I Can...

- [ ] read the 1st sentence.
- [ ] read the 2nd sentence.
- [ ] make a sentence from a picture.
- [ ] color a picture.
- [ ] Draw a picture.

I have three buttons on my dress.

Három gomb van a ruhámban.

The number "three" is saying you got 3 out of 3.

A "három" azt mondja, hogy 3-ból 3-at kapsz.

Name

## I Can...

- [ ] read the 1st sentence.
- [ ] read the 2nd sentence.
- [ ] make a sentence from a picture.
- [ ] color a picture.
- [ ] Draw a picture.

I have 0 tails.

0 farkam van.

The number "zero" is saying, Ok.

A "nulla" szám azt mondja, rendben.

Name ____________

## I Can...

- [ ] read the 1st sentence.
- [ ] read the 2nd sentence.
- [ ] make a sentence from a picture.
- [ ] color a picture.
- [ ] Draw a picture.

I have five fingers on 1 of my hands.

Az egyik kezem öt ujjam van.

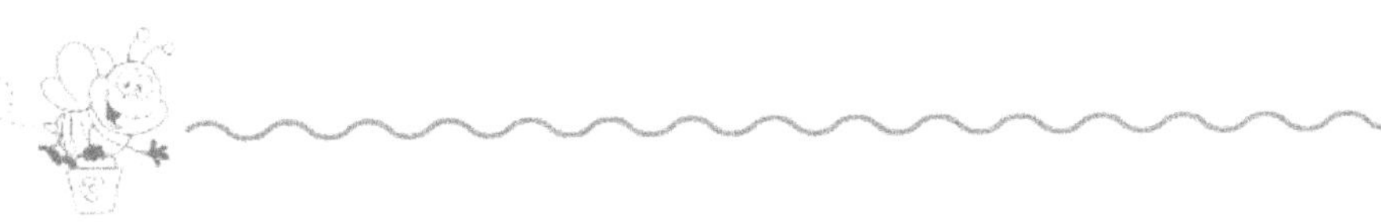

The number "five" is trying to give you a high five.

Az "öt" szám próbál magas neked adni.

Name

## I Can...

- [ ] read the 1st sentence.
- [ ] read the 2nd sentence.
- [ ] make a sentence from a picture.
- [ ] color a picture.
- [ ] Draw a picture.

My cat has four legs.

A macskámnak négy lába van.

_______________________________

The number "four" is counting to four.

A "négy" szám négyre növekszik.

Name

## I Can...

- [ ] read the 1st sentence.
- [ ] read the 2nd sentence.
- [ ] make a sentence from a picture.
- [ ] color a picture.
- [ ] Draw a picture.

A butterfly has six legs.

A pillangónak hat lába van.

The number "six" is saying 1+5=6.

A "hat" szám azt jelenti, hogy 1 + 5 = 6.

Name

## I Can...

- [ ] read the 1st sentence.
- [ ] read the 2nd sentence.
- [ ] make a sentence from a picture.
- [ ] color a picture.
- [ ] Draw a picture.

A spider has eight legs.

A póknak nyolc lába van.

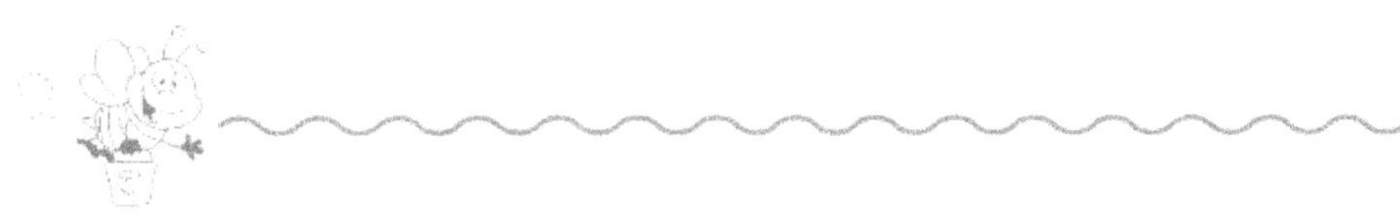

The happy and excited eight is holding up eight fingers

A boldog és izgatott nyolc ujját tartja fel

Name

## I Can...

- [ ] read the 1st sentence.
- [ ] read the 2nd sentence.
- [ ] make a sentence from a picture.
- [ ] color a picture.
- [ ] Draw a picture.

The rooster is going to wake people up.

A kakas felébreszti az embereket.

The rooster is on the fence.

A kakas a kerítésen van.

## I Can...

- [ ] read the 1st sentence.
- [ ] read the 2nd sentence.
- [ ] make a sentence from a picture.
- [ ] color a picture.
- [ ] Draw a picture.

My sister has nine stuffed animals.

A nővéremnek kilenc kitömött állata van.

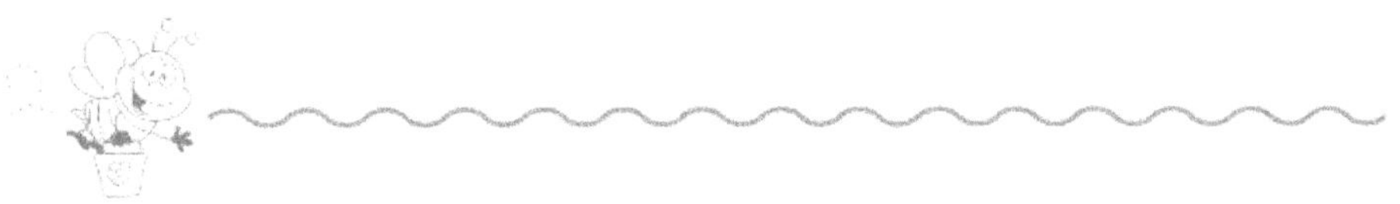

The smiling number nine is saying its name out loud.

A mosolygó kilencedik szám hangosan mondja ki a nevét.

Name

## I Can...

- [ ] read the 1st sentence.
- [ ] read the 2nd sentence.
- [ ] make a sentence from a picture.
- [ ] color a picture.
- [ ] Draw a picture.

The baby bee has yellow and black stripes.

A méhecske sárga és fekete csíkokkal rendelkezik.

The bee is wearing a pink pacifier to calm itself.

A méh rózsaszínű cumi visel, hogy megnyugtassa magát.

Name

## I Can...

- ☐ read the 1st sentence.
- ☐ read the 2nd sentence.
- ☐ make a sentence from a picture.
- ☐ color a picture.
- ☐ Draw a picture.

The ladybug has many spots.

A katicabogár sok folttal rendelkezik.

The red and black ladybug is just done eating some leaves.

A vörös és fekete katicabogár éppen annyit tesz, hogy néhány levelet eszik.

Name

## I Can...

- [ ] read the 1st sentence.
- [ ] read the 2nd sentence.
- [ ] make a sentence from a picture.
- [ ] color a picture.
- [ ] Draw a picture.

The sheep are skinny.

A juhok vékonyak.

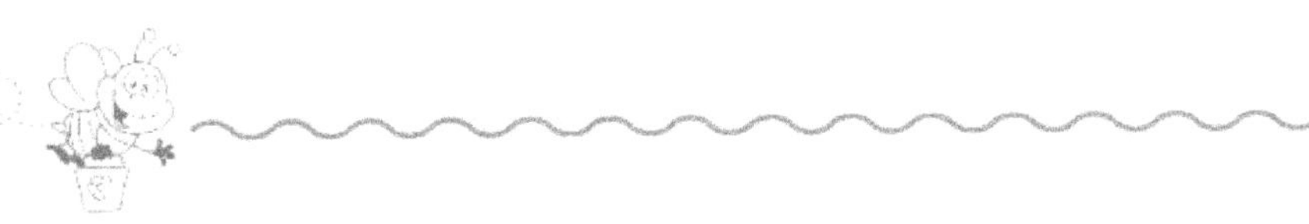

The white sheep have a lot of fluffy white wool to give away.

A fehér juhoknak sok bolyhos fehér gyapjú van, amit odaadnak.

Name 

## I Can...

- [ ] read the 1st sentence.
- [ ] read the 2nd sentence.
- [ ] make a sentence from a picture.
- [ ] color a picture.
- [ ] Draw a picture.

The rabbit is entering an egg painting contest.

A nyúl tojásfestési versenyre lép.

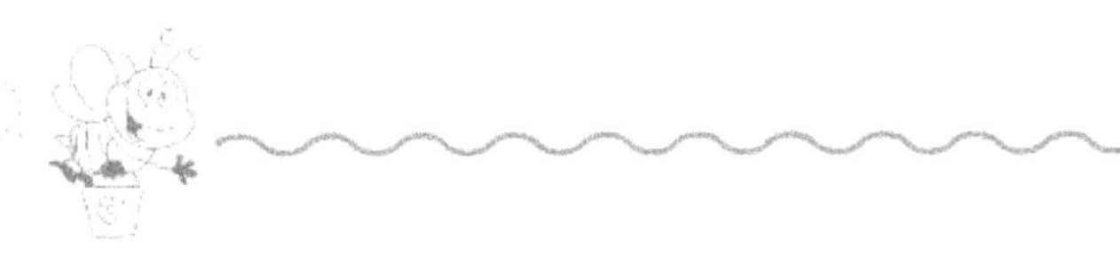

The Easter Bunny is painting a chocolate egg.

A húsvéti nyuszi csokoládétojást festett.

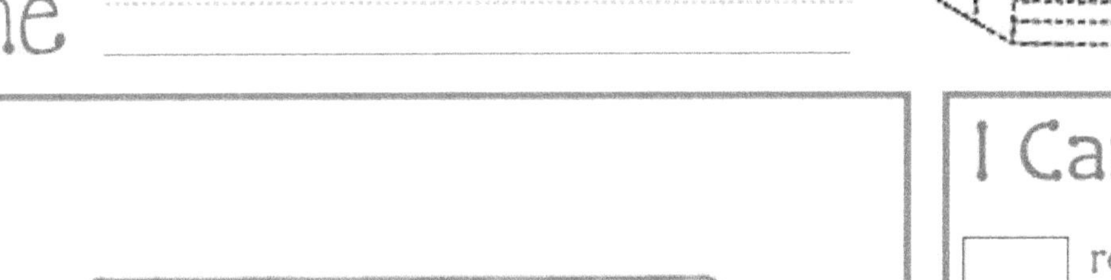

The owl is a language arts teacher.

A bagoly nyelvtanár.

An owl is teaching the kids in school about work.

Egy bagoly tanítja a gyerekeket az iskolában a munkáról.

Name

## I Can...

- [ ] read the 1st sentence.
- [ ] read the 2nd sentence.
- [ ] make a sentence from a picture.
- [ ] color a picture.
- [ ] Draw a picture.

The man has an ancient hammer.

Az embernek ősi kalapácsa van.

The builder man has gone to work on a project.

Az építő ember dolgozott egy projekten.

Name

## I Can...

- [ ] read the 1st sentence.
- [ ] read the 2nd sentence.
- [ ] make a sentence from a picture.
- [ ] color a picture.
- [ ] Draw a picture.

The goat has a friend.

A kecskenek van egy barátja.

The old goat is proud of its golden bell.

Az öreg kecske büszke arany harangjára.

Name

## I Can...

- [ ] read the 1st sentence.
- [ ] read the 2nd sentence.
- [ ] make a sentence from a picture.
- [ ] color a picture.
- [ ] Draw a picture.

My mom's friend is a maid.

Anyám barátja egy szobalány.

The maid is going to clean the hotel room.

A szobalány megtisztítja a szállodai szobát.

Name

## I Can...

- [ ] read the 1st sentence.
- [ ] read the 2nd sentence.
- [ ] make a sentence from a picture.
- [ ] color a picture.
- [ ] Draw a picture.

I went to the zoo.

Elmentem az állatkertbe.

The animals are having a big celebration.

Az állatok nagy ünnepet tartanak.

Name

## I Can...

- [ ] read the 1st sentence.
- [ ] read the 2nd sentence.
- [ ] make a sentence from a picture.
- [ ] color a picture.
- [ ] Draw a picture.

The dinosaur has a pillow.

A dinoszaurusznak van párna.

The dragon is using the rock to build its house.

A sárkány a sziklát használja a ház építéséhez.

Name

## I Can...

- [ ] read the 1st sentence.
- [ ] read the 2nd sentence.
- [ ] make a sentence from a picture.
- [ ] color a picture.
- [ ] Draw a picture.

The boy is excited to go to school.

A fiú izgatottan jár iskolába.

The boy is late for school, so he is sprinting.

A fiú késik az iskolában, tehát sprint.

Name

## I Can...

- [ ] read the 1st sentence.
- [ ] read the 2nd sentence.
- [ ] make a sentence from a picture.
- [ ] color a picture.
- [ ] Draw a picture.

The kids on the school bus are going to school.

Az iskolabusz gyerekei iskolába mennek.

The children are going on a field trip on the yellow bus.

A gyerekek terepi kirándulást folytatnak a sárga buszon.

Name ____________________ 77

## I Can...

- [ ] read the 1st sentence.
- [ ] read the 2nd sentence.
- [ ] make a sentence from a picture.
- [ ] color a picture.
- [ ] Draw a picture.

The cobra is very lovely.

A kobra nagyon kedves.

~~~~~~~~~~~~~~~~~~~~~~~~~~~~~~~~~~~~~

The rattlesnake is looking for its dinner.

A csörgő kígyó vár vacsorára.
~~~~~~~~~~~~~~~~~~~~~~~~~~~~~~~~~~~~~

Name ______________________

## I Can...

- [ ] read the 1st sentence.
- [ ] read the 2nd sentence.
- [ ] make a sentence from a picture.
- [ ] color a picture.
- [ ] Draw a picture.

That is a fat dog!

Ez egy kövér kutya!

~~~~~~~~~~~~~~~~~~~~~~~~~~~~~~~~~~

This dog is wagging its tail for more treats.

Ez a kutya a háta mögött vonzza a további kezeléseket.
~~~~~~~~~~~~~~~~~~~~~~~~~~~~~~~~~~

Name

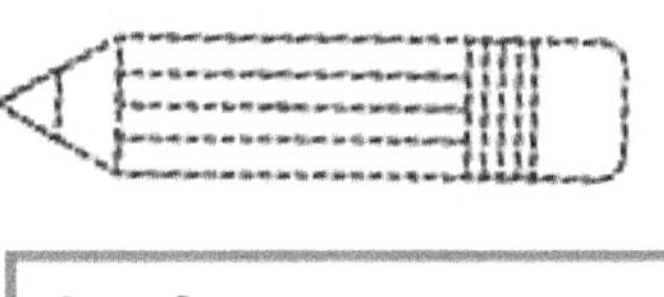

## I Can...

- [ ] read the 1st sentence.
- [ ] read the 2nd sentence.
- [ ] make a sentence from a picture.
- [ ] color a picture.
- [ ] Draw a picture.

The elephant lives in the zoo.

Az elefánt az állatkertben él.

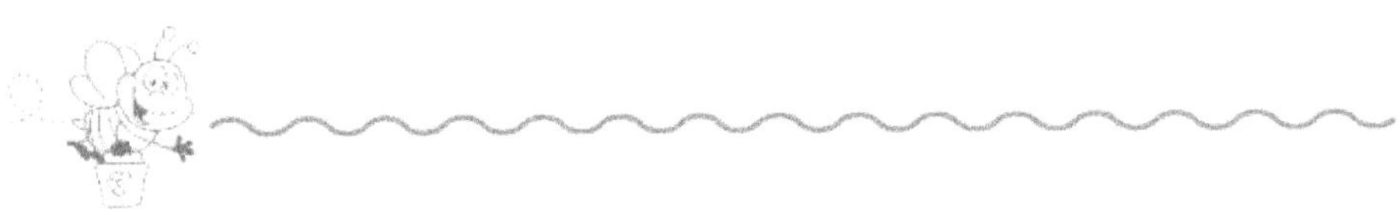

The elephant has a long trunk to spray water.

Az elefántnak hosszú törzse van a víz permetezésére.

Name

## I Can...

- [ ] read the 1st sentence.
- [ ] read the 2nd sentence.
- [ ] make a sentence from a picture.
- [ ] color a picture.
- [ ] Draw a picture.

The giraffe eats vegetables.

A zsiráf zöldségeket eszik.

The giraffe has an extremely long neck.

A zsiráfnak rendkívül hosszú nyaka van.

Name ____________________

## I Can...

- [ ] read the 1st sentence.
- [ ] read the 2nd sentence.
- [ ] make a sentence from a picture.
- [ ] color a picture.
- [ ] Draw a picture.

The chipmunk has a soft tummy.

A mókus puha hasával rendelkezik.

___________________________________

The Chipmunk is about to eat a brown acorn.

A mókus hamarosan barna makkot fog enni.

Name

## I Can...

- [ ] read the 1st sentence.
- [ ] read the 2nd sentence.
- [ ] make a sentence from a picture.
- [ ] color a picture.
- [ ] Draw a picture.

I have ten toes in total.

Összesen tíz lábujjam van.

The one and the zero are holding hands.

Az egyik és a nulla kézen fogva állnak.

Name 

## I Can...

- ☐ read the 1st sentence.
- ☐ read the 2nd sentence.
- ☐ make a sentence from a picture.
- ☐ color a picture.
- ☐ Draw a picture.

The alligator is jumping.

Az aligátor ugrik.

The crocodile is excited.

A krokodil izgatott.

Name

## I Can...

- [ ] read the 1st sentence.
- [ ] read the 2nd sentence.
- [ ] make a sentence from a picture.
- [ ] color a picture.
- [ ] Draw a picture.

I found an ant.

Találtam egy hangyát.

The ant is telling a story.

A hangya egy történetet mesél.

Name

## I Can...

- [ ] read the 1st sentence.
- [ ] read the 2nd sentence.
- [ ] make a sentence from a picture.
- [ ] color a picture.
- [ ] Draw a picture.

The bat sleeps upside down.

A denevér fejjel lefelé alszik.

The bat is ready to fly.

A denevér kész repülni.

Name ____________

## I Can...

- ☐ read the 1st sentence.
- ☐ read the 2nd sentence.
- ☐ make a sentence from a picture.
- ☐ color a picture.
- ☐ Draw a picture.

The cat is very tired.

A macska nagyon fáradt.

The cat is taking a nap.

A macska alszik.

Name

## I Can...

- [ ] read the 1st sentence.
- [ ] read the 2nd sentence.
- [ ] make a sentence from a picture.
- [ ] color a picture.
- [ ] Draw a picture.

The dog likes to play.

A kutya szereti játszani.

The dog is playing with a bone.

A kutya csonttal játszik.

Name 

## I Can...

- ☐ read the 1st sentence.
- ☐ read the 2nd sentence.
- ☐ make a sentence from a picture.
- ☐ color a picture.
- ☐ Draw a picture.

The elephant has eyelashes.

Az elefántnak szempillája van.

The elephant is shy.

Az elefánt félénk.

Name

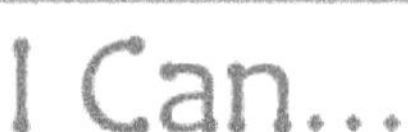

## I Can...

- [ ] read the 1st sentence.
- [ ] read the 2nd sentence.
- [ ] make a sentence from a picture.
- [ ] color a picture.
- [ ] Draw a picture.

The frog is hopping.

A béka ugrál.

The frog is trying to catch the fly.

A béka megpróbálja elkapni a légyet.

Name

## I Can...

- [ ] read the 1st sentence.
- [ ] read the 2nd sentence.
- [ ] make a sentence from a picture.
- [ ] color a picture.
- [ ] Draw a picture.

The goat is sleepily walking around.

A kecske álmosan járkál.

The goat is eating grass.

A kecske füvet eszik.

Name

## I Can...

- [ ] read the 1st sentence.
- [ ] read the 2nd sentence.
- [ ] make a sentence from a picture.
- [ ] color a picture.
- [ ] Draw a picture.

The hippo has a big head.

A vízilónak nagy feje van.

The hippo has a big head.

A vízilónak nagy feje van.

Name

## I Can...

- ☐ read the 1st sentence.
- ☐ read the 2nd sentence.
- ☐ make a sentence from a picture.
- ☐ color a picture.
- ☐ Draw a picture.

The iguana has a long tail.

Az iguánának hosszú farka van.

The iguana is hiding behind the letter I.

Az iguána az I. betű mögött rejtőzik.

# Name

## I Can...

- [ ] read the 1st sentence.
- [ ] read the 2nd sentence.
- [ ] make a sentence from a picture.
- [ ] color a picture.
- [ ] Draw a picture.

Mom bought a new bottle of jam.

Anya vett egy új üveg lekvárt.

There is jam on the bread.

Van lekvár a kenyéren.

Name

## I Can...

- [ ] read the 1st sentence.
- [ ] read the 2nd sentence.
- [ ] make a sentence from a picture.
- [ ] color a picture.
- [ ] Draw a picture.

The kite has a beautiful tail.

A sárkánynak gyönyörű farka van.

The kite is on the ground.

A sárkány a földön van.

Name

## I Can...

- [ ] read the 1st sentence.
- [ ] read the 2nd sentence.
- [ ] make a sentence from a picture.
- [ ] color a picture.
- [ ] Draw a picture.

The lion is timid.

Az oroszlán félénk.

The lion is big.

Az oroszlán nagy.

Name

## I Can...

- [ ] read the 1st sentence.
- [ ] read the 2nd sentence.
- [ ] make a sentence from a picture.
- [ ] color a picture.
- [ ] Draw a picture.

I like mice.

Szeretem az egereket.

A rat is on top of the letter M

Egy patkány van az M betű tetején

Name

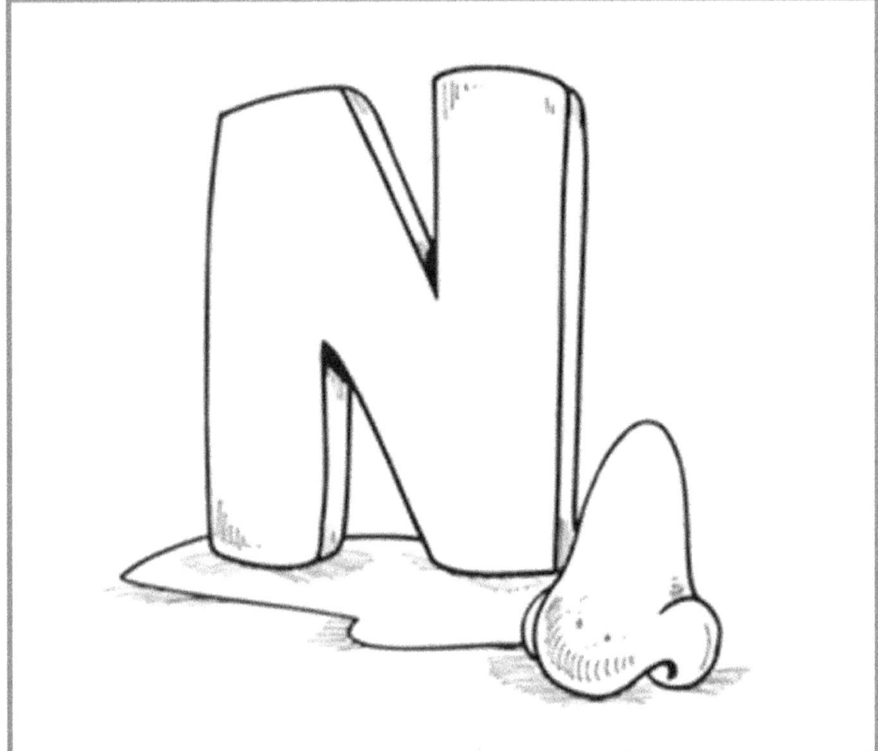

## I Can...

- [ ] read the 1st sentence.
- [ ] read the 2nd sentence.
- [ ] make a sentence from a picture.
- [ ] color a picture.
- [ ] Draw a picture.

The nose is breathing.

Az orr lélegzik.

The letter N stands for a nose.

Az N betű orrot jelent.

Name

## I Can...

- [ ] read the 1st sentence.
- [ ] read the 2nd sentence.
- [ ] make a sentence from a picture.
- [ ] color a picture.
- [ ] Draw a picture.

The octopus lives underwater.

A polip víz alatt él.

The octopus has eight tentacles.

A polip nyolc csápja van.

Name _______________________

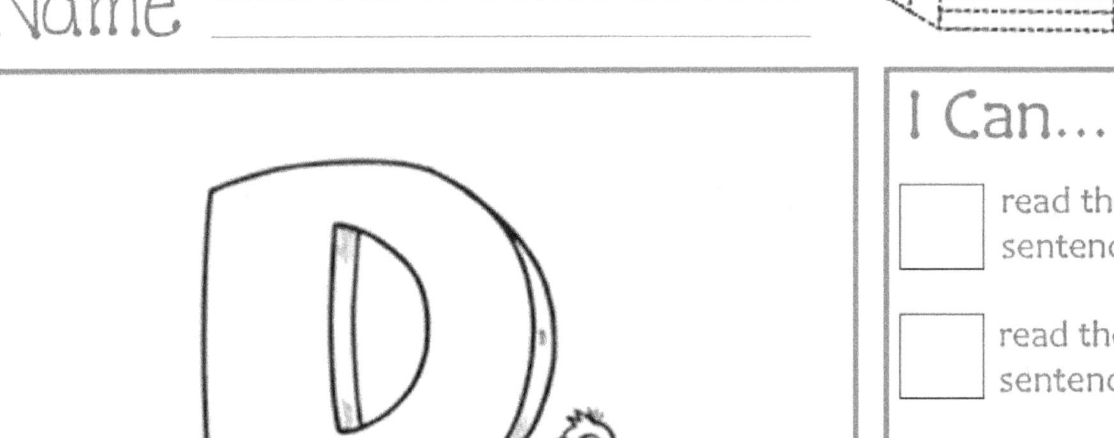

## I Can...

- [ ] read the 1st sentence.
- [ ] read the 2nd sentence.
- [ ] make a sentence from a picture.
- [ ] color a picture.
- [ ] Draw a picture.

The penguin eats fish.

A pingvin halat eszik.

_______________________________

The penguin lives in the arctic.

A pingvin a sarkvidéken él.

Name

## I Can...

- [ ] read the 1st sentence.
- [ ] read the 2nd sentence.
- [ ] make a sentence from a picture.
- [ ] color a picture.
- [ ] Draw a picture.

The queen has a wand.

A királynőnek pálca van.

The queen is beautiful.

A királynő gyönyörű.

Name

## I Can...

- [ ] read the 1st sentence.
- [ ] read the 2nd sentence.
- [ ] make a sentence from a picture.
- [ ] color a picture.
- [ ] Draw a picture.

The rabbit has long ears.

A nyúlnak hosszú füle van.

The rabbit is thinking about something.

A nyúl gondolkodik valami.

Name

## I Can...

- [ ] read the 1st sentence.
- [ ] read the 2nd sentence.
- [ ] make a sentence from a picture.
- [ ] color a picture.
- [ ] Draw a picture.

The snake has polka dots.

A kígyó pöttyös.

The snake is licking its lip because it is hungry.

A kígyó nyalta az ajkát, mert éhes.

Name

## I Can...

- [ ] read the 1st sentence.
- [ ] read the 2nd sentence.
- [ ] make a sentence from a picture.
- [ ] color a picture.
- [ ] Draw a picture.

The tortoise has a pointy shell.

A teknős hegyes héjú.

The turtle has a robust shell but is very slow.

A teknős robusztus héjú, de nagyon lassú.

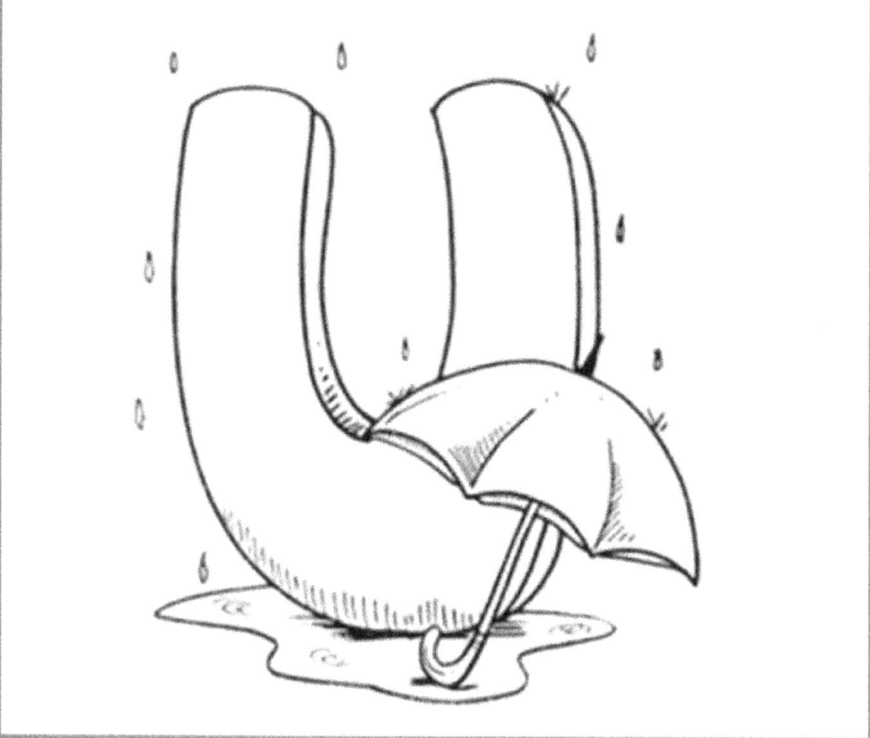

## I Can...

- [ ] read the 1st sentence.
- [ ] read the 2nd sentence.
- [ ] make a sentence from a picture.
- [ ] color a picture.
- [ ] Draw a picture.

It's raining.

Esik az eső.

~~~~~~~~~~~~~~~~~~~~~~~~~~~~~~~~~~~~~~~~~~

We use the umbrella when it's raining.

Esernyőt használunk, amikor esik.
~~~~~~~~~~~~~~~~~~~~~~~~~~~~~~~~~~~~~~~~~~

Name ___________________

## I Can...

- [ ] read the 1st sentence.
- [ ] read the 2nd sentence.
- [ ] make a sentence from a picture.
- [ ] color a picture.
- [ ] Draw a picture.

The violin is a musical instrument.

A hegedű egy hangszer.

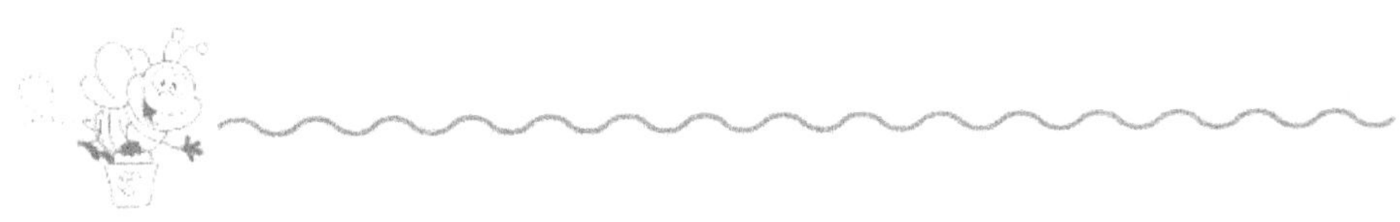

A violin can play beautiful music if played correctly.

Egy hegedű gyönyörű zenét játszhat, ha helyesen játsszák.

Name

## I Can...

- ☐ read the 1st sentence.
- ☐ read the 2nd sentence.
- ☐ make a sentence from a picture.
- ☐ color a picture.
- ☐ Draw a picture.

The walrus has a friend.

A rozmárnak van egy barátja.

The walrus has unusually sharp teeth.

A rozmának szokatlanul éles fogai vannak.

Name ___________

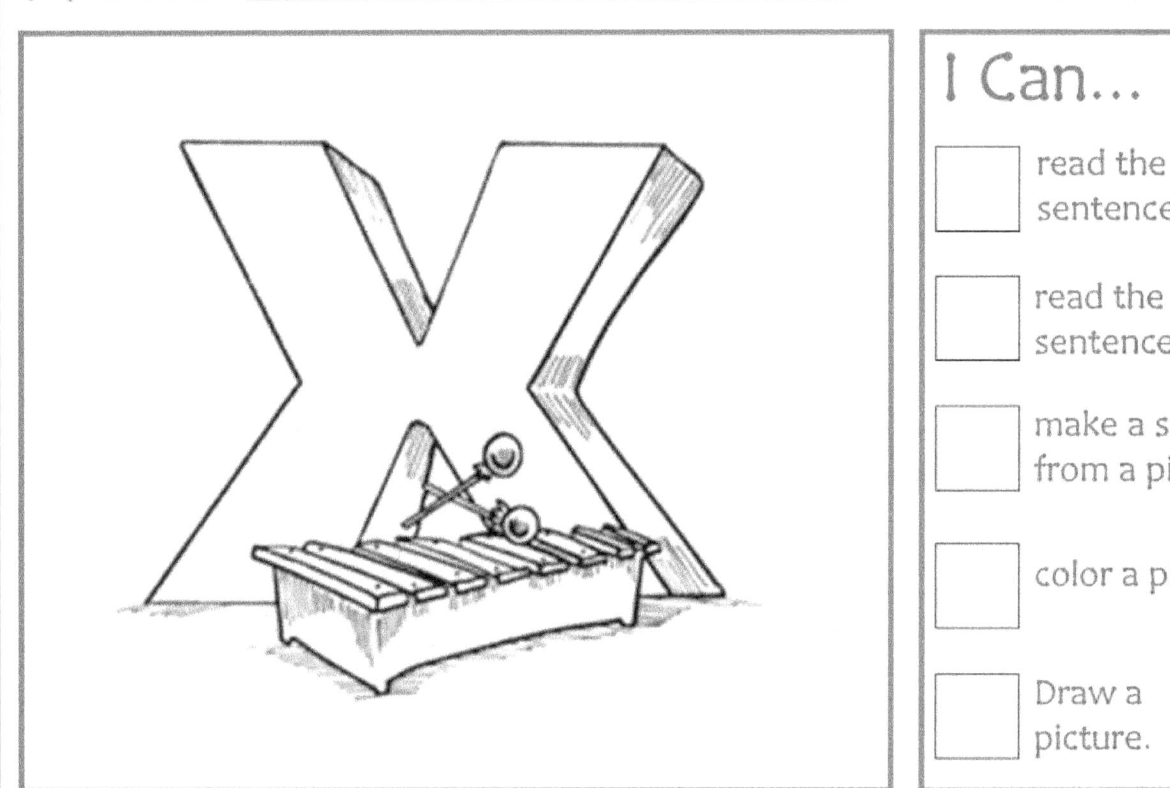

## I Can...

- [ ] read the 1st sentence.
- [ ] read the 2nd sentence.
- [ ] make a sentence from a picture.
- [ ] color a picture.
- [ ] Draw a picture.

The xylophone is a colorful instrument.

A xilofon színes eszköz.

The xylophone is an instrument like the piano.

A xilofon olyan eszköz, mint a zongora.

## I Can...

- [ ] read the 1st sentence.
- [ ] read the 2nd sentence.
- [ ] make a sentence from a picture.
- [ ] color a picture.
- [ ] Draw a picture.

The boy has a little hat.

A fiúnak van egy kis kalapja.

 ________________________________

The boy is having fun playing with a yoyo.

A fiúnak szórakozni játszik egy yoyóval.

Name

## I Can...

- [ ] read the 1st sentence.
- [ ] read the 2nd sentence.
- [ ] make a sentence from a picture.
- [ ] color a picture.
- [ ] Draw a picture.

The zebra has a tail.

A zebrának van farka.

The zebra has black and white stripes.

A zebrán fekete-fehér csíkok vannak.

Name

## I Can...

- [ ] read the 1st sentence.
- [ ] read the 2nd sentence.
- [ ] make a sentence from a picture.
- [ ] color a picture.
- [ ] Draw a picture.

I have a candle on my cake.

Van egy gyertyám a tortámon.

I had a small birthday cake for my party.

Volt egy kis születésnapi torta a partámhoz.

Name

## I Can...

- [ ] read the 1st sentence.
- [ ] read the 2nd sentence.
- [ ] make a sentence from a picture.
- [ ] color a picture.
- [ ] Draw a picture.

The astronaut is going on a mission.

Az űrhajós küldetést folytat.

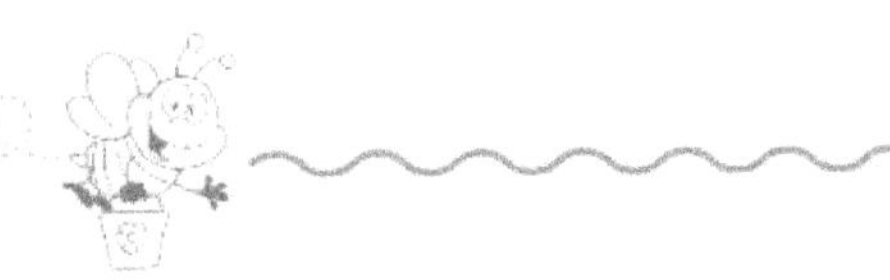

An astronaut has to explore our universe so that we would have more knowledge.

Egy űrhajósnak fel kell fedeznie világegyetemünket, hogy több tudásunk legyen.

## I Can...

- [ ] read the 1st sentence.
- [ ] read the 2nd sentence.
- [ ] make a sentence from a picture.
- [ ] color a picture.
- [ ] Draw a picture.

The samurai is going for a morning jog.

A szamuráj reggel kocogni megy.

The samurai is training to become good at fighting.

A szamuráj edzik, hogy jól harcoljon.

Name ___________________

## I Can...

- [ ] read the 1st sentence.
- [ ] read the 2nd sentence.
- [ ] make a sentence from a picture.
- [ ] color a picture.
- [ ] Draw a picture.

My friend is having a gigantic cake.

A barátomnak van egy hatalmas tortája.

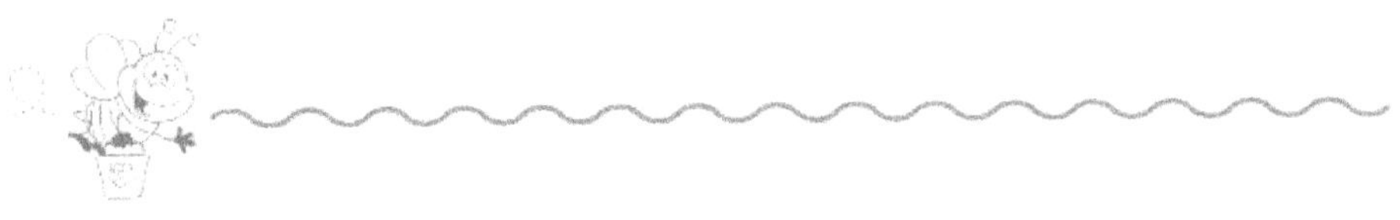

I had a humongous birthday cake for my celebration.

Hatalmas születésnapi torta volt az ünnepemre.

Name

## I Can...

- [ ] read the 1st sentence.
- [ ] read the 2nd sentence.
- [ ] make a sentence from a picture.
- [ ] color a picture.
- [ ] Draw a picture.

The frog is chasing the fly.

A béka üldözi a légyt.

The green frog is trying to catch the fly.

A zöld béka megpróbálja elkapni a légyet.

Name 

## I Can...

- [ ] read the 1st sentence.
- [ ] read the 2nd sentence.
- [ ] make a sentence from a picture.
- [ ] color a picture.
- [ ] Draw a picture.

The ladybug has six legs.

A katicabogár hat lábú.

 ~~~~~~~~~~~~~~~~~~~~~~~~~~~~~~~

The ladybug is on the leaf.

A katicabogár a levélben van.

Name ______________________

## I Can...

- [ ] read the 1st sentence.
- [ ] read the 2nd sentence.
- [ ] make a sentence from a picture.
- [ ] color a picture.
- [ ] Draw a picture.

The dragon is sick.

A sárkány beteg.

The dragon just ate something spicy, so he needed water.

A sárkány csak evett valami fűszeres ételt, így vízre volt szüksége.

Name

## I Can...

- [ ] read the 1st sentence.
- [ ] read the 2nd sentence.
- [ ] make a sentence from a picture.
- [ ] color a picture.
- [ ] Draw a picture.

That is a baby cow.

Ez egy csecsemő tehén.

A little cow is walking around near the barn.

Egy kis tehén sétál körül az istálló közelében.

Name

## I Can...

- [ ] read the 1st sentence.
- [ ] read the 2nd sentence.
- [ ] make a sentence from a picture.
- [ ] color a picture.
- [ ] Draw a picture.

The frog has a big smile.

A béka nagy mosollyal rendelkezik.

The frog is smiling because it is happy.

A béka mosolyog, mert boldog.

Name

## I Can...

- [ ] read the 1st sentence.
- [ ] read the 2nd sentence.
- [ ] make a sentence from a picture.
- [ ] color a picture.
- [ ] Draw a picture.

The frog has a big mouth.

A béka nagy szája van.

The frog is waving to us.

A béka integet nekünk.